Rule the Roost

10 Business Hacks For Indian Market

Ashwini Walia

BlueRose Publishers

First Published in October 2020

ISBN: 978-93-90432-50-9

BLUEROSE PUBLISHERS

www.bluerosepublishers.com

info@bluerosepublishers.com

+91 8882 898 898

Cover Design:

Joshua Freitas

Typographic Design:

Namrata Saini

Distributed by: BlueRose, Amazon, Flipkart, Shopclues

Preface

Born in a Business Family, I have always had the curiosity to know how businesses continue to prosper and scale even when the competition continues to increase and intensify over time. What keeps a business ticking? The Practices, the Technology, the Passion! After being a part of many small and medium-size organizations, I have been able to wrap my head around the ever-changing business world with some success. Being a part of some successful and some unsuccessful enterprises has taught me that there isn't "one stroke for all folks" strategy for a successful business. It's about adapting to the changes, implementing the strategies and sustaining the turmoil you come across in the fiercely competitive business world. In this book, I have tried to highlight and explain most of the practices that would lead a business on the path to sustained profitability. Time is of essence that's why most of the methods which have been highlighted can be implemented in a short span of time, which could assist one in experiencing the changes at the earliest.

This Book is dedicated to Ms. Raj Rani Jaj (Bua, Aunt), who has stood like a Pillar with me throughout my ups and downs of life. It's not often that one loses his mother at a very young age and finds a genuine soul to guide through the journey of life.

Things to keep in mind while reading this book

First and foremost, thanks a ton for picking up this Book. This book represents over 10 years of my experience being associated with small businesses and my formal education in business management. I have done all that I could to encapsulate all my learnings in less than 100 pages. It's a crisp and smooth ride which will go a long way in assisting you in running your business efficiently and smoothly.

I have made a conscious attempt in this book to not complicate it with complex business tools which can deter a reader from making complete sense with utmost ease. Also, one doesn't need to read the entire book at one go to understand it. I recommend people to go slow and make short notes at the end of each chapter, so the teachings stay with you for a very long time. Each chapter functions like a standalone lesson which if grasped well is a great ROI, to begin with. Sustainability and Innovation are at the core of this book; I request you not to get disturbed by these terms as these have been simplified in the most effective way possible.

The Book has 10 Chapters and 3 Bonus chapters. The 10 chapters comprise of the knowledge, information and practical applications which are required to run a business smoothly. There are some essential business hacks in each chapter with short stories which will make the experience of reading more relatable. The book is organized keeping in mind the order in which the essentials one needs to grasp and can grasp with ease. Yet, if someone wishes to read the book from any chapter of their choice feel free as each chapter by itself has the necessary ingredients to make a topic understandable to its fullest. The Bonus chapters are about the important learnings which I have acquired from some of the finest human-beings I have been lucky enough to witness in my lifetime, Simon Sinek and Sachin Tendulkar to name a few.

It's a Book-Diary, which means as a business professional it should stay with you at all times, almost. Again, after each chapter I have left a blank page for you to strategize and brainstorm new ideas. Remember to make the most of it. I have also left my contact details if there is anything (related to the book or your business) you wish to discuss email it to me; my team and I would be more than happy to assist you on the matter. Happy Reading!

Contents

Google it!

What's the first thing that comes to mind when someone says I have an issue at hand, how do I resolve it, we almost every time say, 'Google it', isn't it! Small Businesses in India are slowly but surely falling in love with technology. It's still a reasonably new quadrant for the small business owners to explore, but the spirit seems to be fresher than ever. And not to anyone's surprise, Google is ensuring everything it can do to blow this segment wide open so that one can start maximizing the gains. I will not walk you through the history of it; in fact, we will dive straight into how this is happening and what can a small business expect from countless tools that Google has to offer. I had conducted a small survey in Delhi NCR region of India and not to my surprise most SMEs were not aware of 80% plus applications and services currently being offered by Google which can directly help these businesses increase their top line with little effort.

Google Search Engine (SE) – We know this tool as the holy grail of information. The amount of information it can provide us is unimaginable but not many people are aware of the fact that one can advertise on this platform and do wonders to their business, no matter how small or big the company. It all starts with SEO, Search Engine Optimization. The

Process to get traffic to your website organically. Let's understand this in brief.

Search Engine Optimization (SEO) - SEO is an organized process to improve your organic (non-paid) ranking in an online search. SEO is sometimes referred to as organic search, free search or natural search. Whatever you call it, it's all about how your website ranks in the list of search results when someone searches for your product or service.

Small Businesses, mostly devoid of funds, this can be your long-term friend who has your back at all times. Just like any other long-term relationship, you will need to nurture it.

Here is how you can improve your Search Engine Ranking:

- Viewable – Ensure your site can be viewed across any and all devices: phones, tablets and laptops. Your site should be optimized, responsive and user-friendly. Site speed and load time can also impact the SEO process.
- Secure – Make it a point on not missing out on https, especially if you require sensitive information or have e-commerce functions.
- Images – Search engines crawl your images within your website. Make sure all of your images have "alt text", and image files are named appropriately. For example, "red convertible car" is better than "image_13."
- Content – Write content that people find useful. Useful content gets shared, spreading your content across Twitter, blogs and other social media.

Quality is more important than the quantity of content. Make sure your content includes keywords or phrases that reflect what you do and how users search for you.

- Links – Include inbound and outbound links on your site. When one-page links to another, it usually indicates to the search engines that this site has valuable information. Be careful though, only send people to trustworthy websites and make sure anyone linking to you is also reliable.
- Titles – Include unique meta-titles and descriptions for each page on your site. Think about meta-titles as chapters of a book — they summarize the contents of each page. For instance, "Burger delivery area" is better than "burg3b." Make sure your URL structure is user friendly too. For example, "/blog/tips-for-SEO" vs. "/blog/read22."

"For many people google is the most important tool on the web" – Merissa Mayer, Businesswoman, Investor and cofounder of Lumi Labs.

#Locallypromoteyourbusiness

Google My Business (GMB) – Why you need a Google My Business Listing?

Google has reported that a staggering 46% of all searches have local intent (Source: Search Engine Round Table). Yet, despite this information, there are plenty of businesses which fail to take advantage of the free-to-use Google My Business platform. There are several perks of getting set up on GMB, so whether you're considering creating a listing for your business or looking for the best ways to boost your local presence, make sure your company shows up on GMB.

Harness the power of GMB

- Increase brand awareness
- Tap the local market
- Earn customer's trust through reviews
- Increase traffic and sales through organic and inorganic traffic flow
- Communicate with your customers
- Drive your business with data-driven insights
- Create Ads and Posts

How to Optimize GMB

1. Complete your business information and add a description
2. Upload more and better images
3. Respond to Google My Business reviews (yes, all of them)
4. Use posts to promote events, offers, and content
5. Create and upload videos

Capture Leads

Google Forms - All Businesses run on leads/footfalls/Inquiries, and therefore having a lead management system in place is critical. Big company's employ costly, proven software's for the same which are expected to work as highlighted. But it's not a hard and fast rule that these software yield the desired results or even close to it. On the other hand, small companies often don't have big budgets to buy these software, but that very hurdle is no longer a roadblock. With many alternatives now being sold for a low price or almost free of cost deploying a lead capture system is not that big a hurdle. But, if you function without one, you are inviting trouble. Google provides one such free tool, Google Forms, which are not only easy to use but very effective too. Not only can you have these forms to collect leads for you, but it makes the entire process of lead gathering and management look hassle-free. You can design these forms as per your liking and introduce questions which are easy to answer and not intimidating. Above all, you can integrate these forms on your landing pages, website, Facebook page and at places where you may feel it's a necessity. So, next time don't allow leads to leak; proper lead management can lead to higher sales.

Organize your dates with work

Google Calendar – It's good to be organized. It's even better to be effectively organized. It's best to use google calendar, one-stop to ensure you don't miss your appointments, organize your day, week or your minutes, and make alterations at the click of a button. Google Calendar doesn't just take care of your meetings; it also keeps track of notifications, reminders, allows you to speed up your work and integrate tools like Zappier for smoother functioning.

Your website is your identity on digital space

Google Sites – This book will talk about the importance of having a website a number of times. It is your identity, your real estate, your passport to trust-building journey with your customers and a pillar to your plans to build an empire. If you ignore it, it could well be the thorn which brings your company down. Plan it carefully and plan it for the long term.

Now, why Google websites? There are many platforms which give you the tools required to create a website in less than 15 minutes then why google. Well, I am not going to bind you to google sites, but it has its advantages. Before we deep dive let me tell you "go daddy," a website builder and one of the leading website sellers in the market remains a great alternative to google and one can go ahead and utilize it without hesitating but don't ignore google, let's find out why.

5 Key features of Google Sites

1. Create Webpages with minimum hassle – Plenty of themes to choose from, fonts to utilize, easily introduce photos in your site, options to upload documents makes google a quick alternate to many website builders.
2. Utilize google sheets, forms and other google services at the click of a button – You can easily access your google drive for sheets, forms, docs, slides, calendar, maps to ensure all essential tools of your business are seamlessly integrated into your website.
3. Embed External Content – Option to introduce external content with the help of html coding makes the complex task look easy. One doesn't need to be a coder to embed html codes. All one needs to do is copy paste codes using html plugin,

and stuff happens like magic. This is super easy and super-efficient.

4. Intra-site – This is where google triumphs over most. Its security features make it very easy to create internal websites which can only be accessed by people you give the access rights to. You are getting closer to be your company's tech guy with the least amount of effort.
5. Customization and Marketing – You can organize your content with a fair amount of ease and customize it whenever you want without the help of an expert. Plus promoting your website for marketing and advertising has never been this easy. Whether its SEOs or Google Ads, all can be so undemanding that you will get glued to it.

Many More...

Landing Pages, Google Sheets, Google Analytics, Google AdWords, Google Data Studio, G Suite.

Google Advertising, Google My Business and Google Keep – Start your google journey with these apps, and you will soon be experiencing growth you have not imagined before. Once you have gained reasonable control over these, you can start exploring the uncharted territory with greater success.

Google is a world that deserves exploring to the fullest. Falling short in utilizing google to the maximum of your ability will hurt you in the long run. So, pay regular attention to google, all its new integrations and launches should be taken seriously, and one should always think about how best you can integrate these tools into your business.

Strategize

Sell or be Sold

Well, there are books, articles, blogs, vlogs, and what not written and said on this subject but still companies fall short on realizing how important it is for small businesses to not only sell but also have the mindset to sell effectively. Sales is the backbone of every small business irrespective of what people say. Perfect the design first sales will follow, setup your office first sales will eventually happen, blah blah blah sales will come to you, no, never, if you don't sell the product asap there is a good chance you will perish without leaving footprints. Nothing is more damaging to a small business than an underperforming sales quadrant. Up the ante and keep it elevated throughout the journey. Even if you are not a salesperson or don't have the sales mindset, you have to find a way of ensuring sales remain a top agenda in the company at all times. Many sales experts have time and again highlighted that we all keep selling at all times, whether ideas, services or products, to our parents, friends and family, or investors or our teammates, or our employees or customers, sales is a part of our life. But we often fail to sell when it matters the most. Let's see how we can ensure not to fizzle out when the stakes are high.

"How you sell matters. What your process is matters. But how your customers feel when they engage with you matters more." – Tiffani Bova, Global Customer Growth and Innovation Evangelist at Salesforce.

(I) Sales Tools

Entering today's work war zones without digital tools is a practical suicide. No matter what business you are in and no matter what scale you operate at, digital tools function like lifelines. Many companies today have taken a liking for WhatsApp Business as a tool for increasing marketing and sales efforts. One can do broadcasting on WhatsApp, one can build small communities on it, one can also integrate business automation which can enable services like drip marketing that can change the game for small companies. Let's make sure you don't shy away from utilizing some of the most useful free tools on offer in the digital space today. I have seen vegetable vendors use WhatsApp with purpose and ease, then why should anyone else be left wondering how to maximize gains through a chat app.

Free Tools

- **WhatsApp**

WhatsApp Business App Features

1. Business Profiles

WhatsApp Business App allows users to create a business profile with helpful information for their customers like address, phone number, business description, email address, and website. It increases businesses visibility and awareness on the messaging application.

2. Smart Messaging Tools

"Quick Replies" – This feature saves you time by permitting you to save, use and reuse messages you frequently send to customers. Through this, you can quickly answer common questions in no time. "Automated Messages" -This allows businesses to set an away message when they are unable to answer customer queries by letting customers know when to expect a response. One can also create a greeting message to introduce your business to your potential customers.

3. Messaging Statistics

The messaging statistics feature of the application allows businesses to be able to review simple metrics behind the messages being sent. You can access essential metrics such as how many of your messages were successfully sent, how many were delivered and read.

4. WhatsApp Web

Beside from using the App to send and receive messages from customers, you can also send and receive messages with WhatsApp Business on your desktop or laptop making it more accessible for business especially those with a customer support team.

WhatsApp allows for more.

- **Google Keep**

5 reasons to start using google keep NOW

Effective To-Do List and Task Sharing – List has never been so easy to create on an app. Create a list; it could be a work-related list of tasks to be achieved or a grocery list for the week. You can also add members of your team or family depending upon the nature of the list and can assign some tasks from the list to them. Once done strike out the task or item from the list for everyone to know it's done.

Integration with GMAIL – The App snippet is available on GMAIL which permits you to do document sharing, tasks assigning, note keeping and many other functions which otherwise seem to be cumbersome.

Use Keep as a "smart napkin" - The Android version of Keep allows free-form sketching and hand-written notes, just as you might do on a napkin at a lunch meeting. Do make the most of it as this could be a great substitute to a scratchpad, the one which stays with you digitally.

Instantly capture anything – How often does it happen that you stumble upon a great idea, a brilliant picture or informative audio and you want to make sure it stays with you in an organized manner. Quite often, right. That's where 'Keep' chips in with its one-tap capture. One tap and you're off to the races.

Incubate your ideas and Set reminders - Don't just capture your ideas develop them over time. Creators should make the most of this in Keep. Capture the moment when genius strikes and make sure you set reminders to revisit it whenever needed.

There is more to 'Keep', keep exploring.

- **Emails**

Is email marketing dead? Well, stats say otherwise. Once considered as the best and the only way digital marketing worked, emails, are today finding stiff competition from countless marketing mediums. Many businesses have shunned the use of emails in favour of other mediums and rightly for them, this is a target centred technique. But this doesn't mean it's not doing well or fading away.

Among many benefits of email, we will highlight some primary ones which will instill confidence in you to not give up on emails even one bit.

1. Credibility Builder – People like to engage in business with people they like, know and trust. Email gives you the ability to build credibility with your audience by sharing helpful and informative content.
2. Communication Enhancer – Reliability and Trust are two primary factors for a communication channel to be effective. Emails help companies capitalize on this effectively and efficiently.
3. Credibility Builder for Brands – Today, companies can share a plethora of information which can assist them in brand building activities. Vlogs, Blogs, Offers, Newsletters, Coupons, Birthday wishes, and many more innovative contents can be shared

through emails which can result in building a desirable image for the brand.

4. Sales Booster – Emails give you a new medium to sell. It's not a promotion tool anymore. There are innovative ways with which people have been selling through emails.

Subject Line – Keep it short and enticing. The goal is to pique the interest of your reader, not to sound like a used-car salesman.

Eg. Have you considered (Through/ Recommendation)?

Opening Line – Avoid beginning with, "hi, my name is…" . Remember to start with something impactful.

Eg. I loved your post on ...

Body – This is where you connect your business to your prospect. Come up with something compelling.

Eg. How, if at all, would you like to improve your strategy?

Closing - A strong close to your sales email gives recipients a clear path to action.

Eg. Let's connect for a 20 min call, do let me know the time and day?

Signature – Do not take this lightly. Utilize the power of it to leave an impression. Keep it short, simple, professional and on- brand. Include a link to your online profile of your choice.

Let's be clear: Email marketing is here to stay.

- **Appointment Scheduling**

The reliance of many small businesses on receptionists and secretaries is never-ending. Many business coaches suggest having an assistant with you no matter what as it assists in keeping you organized and scheduling your appointments and many such tasks which one might want to outsource. But that should not prevent you from having an alternative for them, especially when they aren't available. Doctor's rely on secretaries a lot for their appointments with patients. How about patients scheduling their appointments as per your preferred timing without having to talk to someone on the phone. Great, right. That's what many online appointment scheduling tools provide your customers, an opportunity to schedule their appointments. One such tool is 'Calendly' which can be organized and customized as per your convenience and ease. These apps also assist in collecting a fee and managing customer database. Do not ignore these tools without trying them at least once.

These are some of the many apps on offer which can help you elevate the game. The key is to explore more.

Never forget that businesses run on lead capture or footfalls. The more your pipeline is filled with leads (ideally quality leads) the more potential customers can contribute towards your business' topline. Always be on a lookout for more innovative ways to add to your top line.

(II) Sales Mindset

This is a must to running an effective business. I will try my best not to state this umpteen number of times, but this will tilt the game in your favour. When all your departments start selling the overall health of the company gets a boost. Small companies have small teams, and these teams often have to function like a well-oiled machine to make sure the targets are met. Even if a team doesn't have anything to do directly with the sales of the business the team members and managers should figure out a way of directly or indirectly contributing to the business, this will result in higher sales.

Example - A bookstore has sales executives, procurement team, admin team and cashier, the basic core team which looks after a small bookstore. Sales executives are responsible for increasing the sales of this small business, and as an owner, you often look forward to these executives performing or outperforming their targets. At the same time, the cashier has a role to play which can well infuse the necessary boost your topline is looking for. He is often the point of exit in the store and at the time of billing when a customer is psychologically inclined towards making a payment a little effort in cross-selling or upselling can go a long way in ensuring the customer leaves with more than what he/she came for. After all #whodoesn'twantmore!

(III) Never split the difference

Probably the most controversial topic of the book. There are books, articles, blogs which I have thoroughly researched to reach to this contentious conclusion. We are regularly fed with the equation win-win, which often compels us to settle for a little less than we deserve so that it suits all parties involved and it's not a bad deal. How often have we given in to this? An honest answer is most of the time. Was it worth as a seller? Probably never. So, do we continue this trend of luring the customers by giving in time and again or should we put our foot down. Let's explore.

Ways to Negotiate without giving-in:

Active Listening – No getting away from this. If you are not a good listener, there is a very high probability you will lose the sale. Active listening is at the core of successful selling. All techniques of empathizing, understanding will fall flat if you miss your customers' viewpoint and concerns. It has been noticed again and again, probably down to how business schools groom many students, salesmen/saleswomen in India love talking about the brand and pushing for a sale more often than listening to customers' challenges. Change the strategy, change the outcome.

Mirroring – If you ever were looking for a magic trick this is it. Repeat the last three words or the critical ones of what someone has said because we often fear what is different and find comfort in similarity. It ignites the feeling of empathy and bonding, which often leads to them surrendering their strategy to you. Use this often but not every time. Its powers are unparallel.

That's right – The 2 words that can transform any negotiation. If you were looking for an alternative for "yes", I present to you "that's right". Reaching "that's right" in a negotiation creates breakthroughs. Summarize clients/customers concerns to trigger these words. The building blocks of a good summary are a label combined with paraphrasing.

Reality Bend – To maximize the gains in a tough negotiation make sure you persuade the other party that they have something to lose else the deal will not go through.

- Steer their emotions – Start with empathy and audit and acknowledge their fears. Ignite loss aversion emotion, and soon they will jump to a chance to avoid it.
- The other person goes first – Simple, let the other guy speak first. Getting a figure, they have in mind, allows you to toggle the conversation better. I have observed this very strategy multiple times being employed by my bosses and the success rate of it has been phenomenal.
- Art of being odd – Odd numbers have a thoughtfulness to them. Use odd more than even and avoid a number that ends with 0. There is a reason why your shoes almost every time have a price tag that ends with 9 and not 0.
- Element of Surprise – Make the other party feel generous by staking an extreme anchor, and then after their apparent rejection, offering them an utterly unrelated surprise gift.

#smartselling

Strategize

Partnerships

Partnerships have been around forever. There are formal and informal partnerships depending upon the task you engage in. In a partnership there is an agreement between two parties to pursue mutually beneficial objectives. There may or may not be a contract involved, but both parties clearly understand the goals of the alliance and pledge to work together to achieve the desired results. Here are a few examples of how such strategic relationships can help your business.

"For me, it's important to build good partnerships rather than score centuries. Once, you have those partnerships, you will also get centuries." – M.S.Dhoni, 'I am sure I don't need to write about him' :-D .

1) Work towards attracting New Customers

Accessing new markets and attracting new customers is always high on a company's list of things to do. Partnerships are one way of achieving it. This not only saves cost, infrastructure and distribution network to highlight a few, but also introduces products or services to a potential customer which at one point might have felt out of reach.

For example, a bag manufacturing company could partner with a multi-designer store to display their bags on the shelves of the store in exchange for a commission. This way, both companies are not only exposed to potential new customers but also discover new ways of adding to their top line. This arrangement can also add value to both customer sets. Visitors to the store can save time by not having to visit the bag store separately, and the multi-designer store gets the supplies automatically replenished by the bag company that is coming to the place of business regularly.

2) Cost Cutting

Acquiring new customers always involves additional expenditure, which at times for SMEs is a painful and an undoable process. In times like these partnerships can prove to be a massive support call. Saving those extra bucks can go a long way in protecting and nurturing your company's health.

3) Build Brand Awareness

There are multiple ways through which service companies can offer mutually beneficial services to customers. An example is a local car wash company. You must have taken notice of car washing services located in big malls. These companies place a prominent ad in the lobby or parking area suggesting that anyone who has come there to watch a movie or to shop can text them or call them for a "wash while they watch/shop." The car washing services then offer all mall employees a free wash or discount or pay some rent for occupying a small space in the mall or outside the mall. This setup provides the necessary boost to the car wash company for extending their brand.

4) Broaden Product and Service Offerings

For companies which already have a loyal customer base it's always a temptation to introduce new products and services. One way to do so is by partnering with a company that offers complementary products. A good example might be a company which provides computer service partnering with a company that provides audiovisual services.

Every company has its set of products, suppliers, and systems, and they may have very similar customer bases. Sales and service personnel likely understand both technologies. By pooling their resources and cross-training sales and service personnel, they may be able to enhance their product lines with minimal investment in additional inventories or people. This is not only limited to a certain industry but can be very well exercised in multiple domains with reasonable ease and success.

5) Overcome Weaknesses

Businesses often enter in new areas where they do not have a strong local presence. In such a scenario your potential customers will likely wonder about whether or not you can be trusted on your promise. It's a good practice to align yourself with an established company that already has the trust of its customers, this will help you shorten your time to market.

6) Spurt in your Top Line

Finding the right partnerships is a strategic move which will create stability and expansion. When two companies come together, their customer base grows. It helps you convert new customers and also infuses additional new energy in your existing base of customers when they see you doing something new, like entering a new territory or introducing new products. As more customers get added to your data base, and sales go up, your annual revenue starts showing positive growth.

7) Clubbing

Every business has the potential to offer something extra to their customer. For example, businesses which provide catering services might find it beneficial to partner with an events company to create a bundle that both parties can benefit from. As a result, the customer can benefit from the additional service without having to actively look for it. As businesses want to be growing and expanding continually, partnerships can be a crucial way to help do so. They will provide not only their expertise but find ways to assist you in doing so, as you will do the same for them. The mindset in such partnerships is of prime importance. To have someone who continually assists you in growing in ways you would not always be able to do alone can-do wonders to the overall health of your company.

#unitedweprofitdividedweloss

Strategize

Envision it!

It is vital for small businesses to realize that vision and mission statements are not just fancy phrases to please the management. They lend purpose and solidarity to a business. They give direction to your thoughts and allow you to bring alignment in your approach.

A Business Vision is a clear picture of what direction is the business headed.

According to Forbes, employees who find their company's vision to be meaningful have average engagement scores of 68%, while the average for those who don't is down to around 18% – a sizeable difference! Moreover, **about 70% of workers don't understand their company's vision at all**. Not only is this bad for engagement, but if an employee doesn't understand the company vision, they likely don't understand specific goals either. This makes it very difficult to align their work with the overall strategy. Developing and maintaining loyalty in your employees and clients is critical to a business. Even before you communicate with your customers or clients, your company's vision does it on your behalf at levels which you can't possibly fathom.

Harley Davidson

Harley and his childhood friend, Arthur **Davidson**, built their motor-bicycle out of their friend's 10 by 15-foot wooden shed in Milwaukee, Wisconsin. All dreams start small, what decides it becomes big or not is a vision.

Their vision is "To fulfil dreams through the experiences of motorcycling."

Here's a quick formula for writing good vision statements:

Step 1 - The output

Step 2 - The twist

Step 3 - The quantification

Step 4 - The human connection

For example: "Producing and selling locally sourced cakes and pies (Step1) that are; so delicious and satisfying (Step2), that every customer (Step3) who leaves our store does so with a smile (Step4)."

"Where there is no vision the people perish." - Proverbs 29:18

Developing a vision statement (how to write one)

What is a vision? It's neither a mystery nor very straightforward. Simply put, it's a picture of what success will look like at a particular point in time in future. It answers many questions: What's your USP?

What does your organization look like? What's the size? Why should people take you seriously? How do employees, owners and other stake holders feel about the business? How are you making people's life better?

Complete the visioning process, and you'll have a clearly articulated end for your organization—something that won't change every time the market or your mood shifts.

5 things to keep in mind while writing a vision statement

Short - A vision statement should be concise, ideally no longer than a sentence or two. Your team should not find it verbose; short is sweet works like a charm here. The entire team and organization should be able to repeat it and, more importantly, understand it quickly.

Simple – Thumb rule for a vision statement is clarity. It should focus on one primary goal, avoid distractions and should get registered in one's mind easily. Applies to both, customers and employees.

Specific to your business – Try to describe a unique outcome that only you can provide.

Future-Focused – It should clearly state your long-term focus, not just what you want to achieve in the present.

Ambitious – It should not be easy to achieve, at the same time unrealistic ambitions put people off. Your vision statement should be like a challenge, difficult to achieve, but not unrealistic.

IKEA: "To create a better everyday life for the many people."

What are we trying to achieve by writing a compelling vision statement?

- Creating the pinnacle of the funnel, which every significant action we do going forward will ultimately be contributing towards.
- A memorable and inspirational summary that describes our reason for existence as an organization - one that will help to motivate existing employees and even attract high-quality new ones.
- A succinct statement about what our organization is trying to achieve to help third parties such as investors or the media better understand us.
- A 'limiter' that helps us to rule out specific opportunities which do not ultimately contribute to our vision.

#envisionit

Strategize

Leverage Digital Marketing

This should be a no brainer. The world we live in has made this topic a household name. By now I can write books on this subject. Let's discuss some vital points on how the right Digital Marketing approach can change your business for good in the long run.

"Content is fire; social media is gasoline." –Jay Baer, Bestselling Author, Marketing Expert and Founder of Convince & Convert.

Power of Digital Marketing

1. Today digital marketing tactics are the most cost-effective way to market your business.
2. It is the most measurable form of marketing.
3. One of the greatest strengths digital marketing has that it allows you to target your ideal buyers.
4. Today most people are starting their buyer's journey online.
5. Your customers are on social media, and digital marketing helps you reach them.
6. SEO and local SEO helps you reach more qualified buyers online.
7. Digital marketing helps you connect with mobile customers.
8. You can easily and quickly adapt your strategy and tactics for the best results.

9. Digital marketing levels the playing field, allowing your business to be more competitive.

How to make it happen for you

1. Run Digital Ads (Advertisements)

We see digital ads all over the screens of our phones and laptops whenever we log into a website or a search engine, so much so that we have learnt to live with them. These digital ads annoy us at times, and at times, we find them so useful that we end up clicking on them. There are times when these ads prove to be a lifesaver. With this kind of penetration in our life, digital advertisements have become indispensable.

Today's marketing world loves this kind of impact of digital ads, so much so that it often suggests people to invest heavily in these ads and put the traditional way of advertising on the back burner. Cost-effectiveness is one of the few major reasons why digital ads will only increase in use and popularity. These are fast and easy to plan. One doesn't require ideation reruns and locality screening to help make these ads an efficient reality. In fact, hit and trial is also considered affordable when it comes to digital ads. Make sure you run these ads as regularly as possible. These are not only going to bring you revenue but also give insight into competitor analysis and future trends. Don't wait and don't hesitate; this will be your most potent weapon in the marketing world.

2. Analytics – As highlighted before Digital Marketing is the most measurable form of marketing, and you can analyse whenever possible how your ads are performing. Whether it's Google analytics or

Facebook pixels, analysing your ads performance has never been this easy. In fact, doing a short course on analytics will only do you long term favours on how to measure your investments in the ad world. Don't shy away as this marriage could open the doors to higher bottom line joys.

3. Make Decision-makers take the call – The biggest challenge in sales is reaching out to the decision-maker. One often ends up banging his head against influencers, gatekeepers, entry-level executives before the message could reach the right person, decision-maker. And even if the message gets that far the variables like time, trend, the impact may not be in your favour. Digital Ads weed out these unnecessary elements to a large extent which gives you complete control over how you would like to reach out to the decision-maker. Capitalise on it!

4. Use Visuals – Visual Advertising is your best friend. With the focus span of people on an all-time low, it's the visuals which can do magic for you when the words are failing to amuse.

Five Types of visual content are making a difference

Images – Images get far more views than posts without images. Images, original and relevant, add the much-needed flavour and personal touch to an article which compels people to spend extra time on the article. High quality, attractive images are often expensive to purchase or time-consuming to create. Fortunately, with resources such as Canva, you can create unique, captivating images for free with a simplistic drag-and-drop interface. Alternatively, there are an endless amount of excellent quality photos on photo-sharing sites such as Pexels that one can make use of.

Videos – There has never been a more effective way of highlighting problems and offering solutions to those problems in short a span. A well-done video is your master key to capturing your customers imagination and captivating their problem-solving senses. A quality video can uplift your campaign by extra credibility points. There are several studies that suggest a video showcasing solutions to a problem on the landing page can increase conversion rate by 3 times. Types of videos you can choose from are animation, explainer, demonstration, customer testimonials and plenty more. Brainstorm this section and surprise your conversion rate. Do not forget to send me a thank you email ☺.

Infographics – This still finds a place in the corporate world. A powerful B2B marketing tool which can allow you to reach and sell your products to your clients/customers effectively even before they call in. It can draw up complex data and statistics and collate them into a compelling, easily intelligible visual display.

Memes – The Lockdown was a meme fest. Even for those who had not known about the term 'meme' ended up doing some degree of study on it during the lockdown. These are an easy-to-create, quirky form of visual content which are considered very impactful. Creating your own meme is a great way to evoke positive emotions and set yourself apart from your competitors.

Presentations – Old is gold. These may not be as impactful but because of its wider scope, it still settles well with corporates. The best part about the presentations is that it can be easily shared now. A beautifully crafted presentation can be extremely effective at keeping people engaged with your content.

USER Engagement

1. UGC – User Generated Content, as the name suggests the content which the user generates for your business. If leveraged well this could be extremely powerful. This is very similar to word of mouth, but this can be measured and leveraged, and that's what makes it very useful. Any photo, comment, video, testimonial, review posted by a user on your platform or on affiliate or private platforms can assist your marketing campaigns in multiple ways. It's not a fad; in fact, it's been burning brightly for a while. Encouraging users to do so is the first step in the process. Coca-Cola did it in 2016 when it came out with personalized bottles. The campaign "share a coke" took off all over the world. Personalization is one way of doing it; there are many other ways through which you can achieve it. Get the brainstorming sessions going in your company, and you would be surprised what you come up with.
2. Retargeting – You must have experienced certain ads which appear after you visited a website. Well, it's definitely not serendipity. It's retargeting in motion. The best part about retargeting is that it only targets users that have visited your websites

or landing pages. This means these potential customers have already been exposed to your brand. Targeting such a focused group is extremely powerful, economical and impactful. They say first impression is the last impression but with retargeting you get a second chance to make the first impression, and in some cases you get a third, fourth and more. This makes retargeting a must-have strategy for all business owners.

3. Automate – This is Kaizen in real sense. People who don't have a technical background often find automation complex and unachievable. What if I told you this is easy, doable and can forever change the game for you? Will you try it? You should. One just needs to warm up to it. There are many ways through which you can achieve automation, and the best part is there is no endpoint, it's like self-growth, grow at your own pace but don't remain stagnant. To keep it simple start with G-Suite. G Suite is a suite of cloud computing, productivity and collaboration tools, software and products developed by Google. Some of its straightforward advantages are improved team collaboration, enhanced data security and cost saving. Some of the biggest companies in the world, Whirlpool and AN Airways have migrated some of their operations to G Suite. Its cloud-based operations and google integrations are making it very convenient and efficient to run the business from a central point of control. Also, Google Sheets, just like excel, has the power to become your CRM tool, ERP tool and whatnot, though this initially would take some investment of time, but it's cheap

and powerful. Begin with this small transition and stay tuned to my website (www.ashwiniwalia.com) where I will be sharing various ways of achieving this power in the cheapest and easiest way possible.

Strategize

Keep the cost Low

Capital is mostly scares in small businesses. One has to be very careful, at the same time very efficient when it comes to budgeting and spending(investing) funds. Cost reduction is one such method which has been around for ages and companies still love it for a good reason. Reducing costs in your small business and creating processes that will cost you less money over time doesn't have to take a lot of time or even a lot of effort. In many cases, it's about making smarter choices when deciding where to put your small business fund.

"Beware of little expenses. A small leak can sink a big ship." – Benjamin Franklin

- **Operational**

Oh, there is no end to expenditure in businesses unless you know how to control it. Plus, it takes time and effort to invest and save cost. It's of prime importance to a business owner that he/she is not only able to keep it in check but also know how to reduce it.

5 things you can do to cut operating costs

1. Embrace Technology – That's where we all are headed. An environment where technology is going to play a pivotal role. Accounting software, Integrated marketing software, automated excel

sheets (if you decided against investing in ERPs and CRMs) and many such effective and cost-efficient ways of saving cost must be implemented.

2. Start outsourcing – Do not hire people for every task in your company. Learn the art of outsourcing and get comfortable with it. The way you often outsource tax saving to a CA the same way every business has got tasks which can be outsourced. This saves one money and time.
3. Identify inefficiencies – Before it's too late make it a point that loopholes, as many as possible, should be covered. Your goal is to run a well-oiled machine so make sure anything that slows you down or creates unnecessary hurdles should be shunned.
4. Cancel unused services – Often overlooked are small bills which are not required. These go unnoticed because they don't look too harmful initially, but these often come back to bite you. Learn to put your foot down and the services which are not required should be opted out of without hesitation.
5. Go green – Green is the future. More and more environmental compliances are coming into play, as a result it's important to be ahead in this race. It saves money, reusing existing material in creative ways means that fewer dollars are spent purchasing new stock to create products.

- **Marketing**

Traditional methods of selling which have gone obsolete are a sure shot 'no'. There is a tendency to rely on old methods of marketing which were of use in the past but in the cotemporary scenario are of little or no use should be consciously driven out of your marketing strategy. In today's time there are countless ways through which one can identify whether a given 'old fashioned' marketing technique will work or not, make use of such material available and do the necessary tweaks. We have already discussed the ever increasing reliance on social media and online marketing which is proving to be beneficial.

- **HR**

Many small businesses spend a lot of their budget on hiring employees to perform tasks that are labour-intensive and time-consuming yet not adding much value to the business.

Automation enables you to reduce the number of employees needed to handle these tasks and therefore, lower your overhead and increase your profitability. It also allows you to focus on the quality rather than the quantity of your employees so you can hire better talent to fuel growth.

Organize Your Expenses

Looking at your budget everyday could be extremely strenuous exercise. Not only it eats up valuable time but also could prevent you from looking at larger problem areas with your spending. Categorizing your expenses can ensure you quickly identify high-cost areas of your business or spot opportunities for savings. Begin with dividing your expenses into production and overhead categories, putting expenses related to making your product into production and those related to running your company into overhead.

Also create categories for labour within each. Using this simple but effective approach will assist you in reviewing your spending patterns.

General Overhead

Costs such as rent, phones, advertising and cleaning services generally make up your overhead costs which you incur to run your business. These expenses bite you even when you're not producing your product or service. Break these costs down by function, asking your marketing, sales, administration, human resources and information technology managers to submit individual budgets. Your aim is to target costs that you can reduce without decreasing quality. For example, meet with your insurance providers to look at your coverages and deductibles to find potential cost savings. Talk to your utilities providers to look for ways to increase energy efficiency and lower monthly bills. Rebid service contracts each year to get the lowest contracts possible. Make your marketing department track communications to determine your return on investment for each.

Production Overhead

A very delicate department always posing a question to produce more or not. Keep a tab of what it costs to make your product or offer your service and determine if you are receiving the best quality for the materials and supplies you purchase and if you're getting the best prices. If you can't negotiate better prices with suppliers, ask about better credit terms, credits can go a long way assisting a small business in its long term growth. Ask for credits which can lower your interest payments and stretch your payment times. Take a close look at your production scheduling to determine if you can save money by producing inventory using the just-in-time method or if you can operate your facility using shorter hours by stockpiling inventory.

Overhead and Production Labour

With growth comes challenges such as growing staff expenses. More staff needed to carry out more work. Tenured staff is in for their annual raises. Should you invest in older staff which often outpace market value for some positions. Work from Home (WFH), if the lockdown of 2020 has taught us something valuable about WFH it's the experience that it works. Look at telecommuting for new employees if you feel you can get the same quality of worker and productivity while reducing office costs, pay and benefits. Also, the old employees can benefit from WFH and so can the company. Compare the cost of contract work vs. employees for each function you have, and switch from one to the other if your analysis identifies any functions that are costing too much. Look into offering voluntary benefits in lieu of raises.

Production labour costs can be annoying and tricky if not managed well. It requires forecasting, inventory management and labour scheduling to be looked after regularly. These are the three keys to reducing your production labour costs. This requires you to work closely with your sales team to determine frequency of orders. If your product or service has seasons, the time when it sells more and time when it sells less, make sure the production takes place accordingly. Excess inventory can raise your debt-service costs, but reducing labour costs by producing extra inventory might make up for this by decreasing overtime, extra shift or contract labour costs. If labour expense isn't an issue, use the just-in-time method of making inventory, producing product just before you need it to help reduce debt service on materials and supplies purchases.

Goal is to keep your top line and bottom line as high as possible and reducing cost will play a pivotal role in it. So, make the necessary adjustments and keep the cost low.

#bottomsup

Strategize

Selection before Action

"Sometimes, until you do what you shouldn't have done, you least remember what you should have done"

— Ernest Agyemang Yeboah

(I) Clarity

Clarity: The Secret Ingredient to ensuring your business growth. These 3 questions can lead you to establishing clarity.

Why

Why are you doing it? Is it financial freedom, or being your boss is a big incentive, are you a control everything person, these are fantastic goals to have in mind to achieve but is there a more significant goal attached to it. Are you in it to make people's lives better or are you in it to make a big difference to the society? Whatever it is, it has to be bigger than being your boss and being a control junkie. Remember "Why" is going to be your secret ingredient; it will assist you in scaling your business.

Who

Who are you doing this for? An extremely important question to answer. If you are doing this for everyone, think again. Not everyone resonates with your cause and not everyone needs to. You need to find your niche. You need to have clarity in who benefits from your business and how it benefits them. A passion for wellness and a desire to teach people how to be healthier is too broad. You can niche down and teach people how to use food as fuel. It works the same way with all topics.

Once you have established clarity in terms of the audience you're targeting it becomes easier for you to find where they are and figure out the best way to reach them. You can start talking to them in their language and use the messaging they understand and respond to. The more you reach them and speak with the specifics of that tribe, the more your business will grow. Even when you roll out free content, remember to demonstrate clarity and purpose.

Notice how big brands communicate. Their messaging is always targeted. There is a reason why big brands rarely put out offers of sales on goods and services because that's not what their target customers expect or respond to.

Direction

This applies to both life and business; the two go hand-in-hand. If you don't have clarity in your life goals, it will be hard to focus on building your business. You started and are building a business not only to create freedom and financial security in your life but also for a greater good which keeps you inspired and motivated.

What does your dream life look like? What would an ideal day look like if money were no object? Allow your mind to visualize where all this is going. Destination works like target. If you are not aiming at something you might fall for anything. Take some time today to get clarity. Once you have clarity, take some time to reconnect with the vision.

(II) Critical things first, the 80-20 rule

If you are an entrepreneur and you don't know this magic mantra, then your process of scaling up has been delayed a little already. Be it time management, resource management, client management or any other task; it's the 20% which takes care of 80%. Invest in more clients/customers who bring you 80% of the revenue, these generally are 20% out of the long list you possess; invest more in growth opportunities which are responsible for 80% of the growth, invest more in employees who assist you in 80% growth. This rule is simple and powerful; make sure to follow it all at times.

(III) Don't be afraid to make changes

Entrepreneurship is a journey; a journey filled with ups and downs, challenges, disappointments, profit and loss, good times and an ever-changing tide which will test you from time to time. There are times when things will not work in your favor. What should you do in these times of unfavorable results, uncertainty, lack of guidance or planning? Make changes wherever necessary. In fact, I resonate with people who have wide and varied life experiences and are consciously aware that change makes you stronger, better, kinder, and more interesting. It makes your life full.

#changeisinevitable

Strategize

People First

It goes without saying people are the reason why any and every business in this world can dream of excelling. It will only be apt for a business to make its human resource a top priority. Taking care of your employees can set the tone of a business. We often see a company which is about people exceeding, excelling and sustaining the test of time over companies which are only about monetary gains.

#peoplecreateprofits

(I) Team

Amongst the most underrated tasks is to build a strong team. Small businesses heavily rely on Business owner's talent and brilliance to run the show. This often leads to underestimating the importance of the staff when it comes to expecting brilliance. As a result, they don't invest in hiring quality people, but if they find one, they don't want to lose that person. One of the pillars of a successful business is its team. Having a loyal, qualified, committed team can do wonders to your business' health, revenue and sustainability. Remember, as a business owner scaling your business is your most important task, and a good team which has your back will allow you to scale your business with utmost focus and ease.

How to build effective teams:

Establish leadership.

If your employees trust your judgement, they will work effectively even when you're not around. Before you can start team building, you need to develop the right kind of leadership skills. This doesn't mean asserting authority, instead, try to foster trust through honesty and transparency. Especially in larger organizations, managers can't be everywhere at once, but if your employees trust your judgement, they will work effectively even when you're not around.

Establish relationships with each of your employees.

One of the most significant advantages of a small business is its small team. This allows for individual interaction regularly. Try to learn more about each member of your team, their skill sets, how they are motivated and their likes and dislikes. This knowledge is invaluable to leaders, as it allows them to match each employee's expertise and competence to specific problems, which will help increase their productivity and job satisfaction. At the same time, all-rounders in a small team can be very beneficial, encourage one to be if he/she has unique skills and talent. Gary Vaynerchuk, best-selling author, speaker, entrepreneur, famously known as Garyvee, rates this little exercise of knowing his employees strengths and weaknesses as one of his biggest strengths and a major reason why his ventures do well.

Also, try to include your employees in the decision-making process wherever possible. Instead of delegating tasks, give your team open-ended projects and allow them to determine the best solution. This will encourage them to cooperate and develop problem-solving skills.

Encourage relationships between your employees.

As your team starts to cooperate more, examine the way they work together and take steps to improve communication, cooperation and trust amongst the group. If there are any conflicts, try to resolve them amicably. Listen to both sides of the argument and act as a mediator. One way to do this is to brainstorm solutions, which helps to empower your employees and may lead to new solutions to the problem.

Foster Teamwork

Smoothly functioning team is half the battle won. The moment there has been an effective working relationship established between your employees make sure you assist them to work together even more effectively. Encourage your team to share information, both amongst themselves and within the wider organisation. Also, try to communicate more with your team. Communication with team goes beyond merely holding meetings, make sure they are included in decision making processes and be open to suggestions and concerns. Often ask about each team member's work and offer assistance where necessary, and doing everything you can to communicate clearly and honestly with your team.

Set ground rules for the team.

Team values and goals are the driving forces which will set the tone for the long-term vision. Evaluating team performance alongside individual performance establishes clarity and purpose. Be sure to include your team in this process, so they know what's required and agree with it.

Managers are evaluated on team performance. As a result team building is one of the primary responsibilities a manager has. It isn't something that can be achieved in a short time and then forgotten. It is an ongoing organic process that you will have to facilitate and guide. As this process unfolds, however, your team members will begin to trust and support one another and share their skill sets and effort in order to complete your organisation's goals more effectively.

"At the end of the day, you bet on people, not strategies." – Lawrence Bossidy, American Author, Retired Chairman of board & Ex-CEO Honeywell, held executive positions at GE.

(II) Influencers

Influencers are gaining more and more importance in today's scenario. Though this is an age old phenomenon where influencers were not hired but rewarded in different ways for spreading the right word about the business, but the same has got more structured today. In marketing, it is a hot topic, especially when considering strategies for increased awareness and interest in your brand.

From newly formed start-ups to major corporations like Coca-Cola and Maybelline, companies everywhere are harnessing the popularity of influencers to promote their products.

The question for everyday entrepreneurs and small businesses is how can they benefit from the trend towards influencer marketing? With the cost of social views soaring and YouTube stars commanding six-figure fees, can regular companies exploit the power of influencers?

How to Create an Affordable Influencer Marketing Strategy

If you want to join the craze for influencer marketing, there's no need to pay millions of dollars. Finding key influencers in your niche is relatively simple, and it's a great way to boost your brand recognition.

- Narrow down on product and services you would like to promote
- Research the social scores of influencers in your market niche
- Set your Parameters
- Start promoting

Become an Influencer to Dominate Your Market Niche

Lot of entrepreneurs are doing this today. With their wealth of knowledge in the domain and their understanding that they are the face of their organization, they are taking up this opportunity to spread the right word about the business. This should eventually be on your list of things to do.

(III) Part-Timers

Often ignored these part-timers are handy people who are looking to learn. These may not be a match made in heaven, but these can ensure when you are in soup, you don't suffer.

Benefits of part-timers

- Greater Flexibility – They are hungry to learn. As a result, they take up all sorts of challenges which can bring them multiple benefits. It's a simple give and take relationship, but often companies take it beyond this because occasionally these folks become future employees.
- Cost-Effective – One doesn't need to pay them a lot; in fact, some people work for free in return for poultry benefits like food and an opportunity to learn. People nowadays often joke that Pyramids were built by interns, not sure how true that is but many companies are making the most of it.
- Seasonal Support – Who doesn't want this. There are many small businesses which are season dependent. It's like a blessing to have the intern pool full all around the year to choose from, saves you unnecessary trouble of employees going on vacations or quitting abruptly.
- Expand the pool of candidates – Future employees often come from the interns who served you well. There is no harm in keeping track of their progress and saving yourself extra bucks by not going after unknown entity.
- Willingness to learn – Their desire to learn often becomes a source of their passion which can assist in maintaining and often boosting a positive environment in the company. Not maximizing this flow of energy is a big miss.

#influencethefuture

Strategize

Effective Presentation

Presenting the information clearly and effectively is a key skill to get the message or opinion across and, today, presentation skills are required in almost every field.

- **VM**

Visual Merchandising

Visually appealing stores always attract more customers. Getting the look and feel of your store right, online and offline, is not a preference but a priority. This is a science which if done well could make a big difference to how people perceive your brand. Visual merchandising is a crucial retail strategy that maximizes the aesthetics of a product with the intent to increase and maximize sales. A visual merchandiser has a big role to play in the look, feel and culture of a brand. If visual merchandising is done well, it can create awareness while simultaneously increasing brand loyalty. Drawing customers into the shop is the no.1 aim of any business. Once you are successful at that then closing sales becomes the priority and all of this is largely dependent on the aesthetic quality of your retail display.

Possibly the single and most important reason to engage and inspire your customers is to encourage them to buy more of your products, increasing your sales, margin and return on space. This engagement process begins even before they have set foot in your store.

Many Elements of VM

Success of VM depends on many factors; this includes the store's appearance, including everything from:

- Lighting
- Signage and packaging
- Uniform and presentation
- Point of sale material and ticketing
- Colours, shapes and various textures

An amalgamation of these elements when done correctly tends to showcase a brand in a bright light which ultimately deepens the customer experience, leading to a positive shopping experience and increased sales.

"Innovation, as I understand it, is both about doing different things as well as doing things differently."
Kiran Mazumdar-Shaw, Biotech Entrepreneur.

- **Website**

Vice President of Marketing, SCORE, said, "If a company or a small business doesn't have an online presence, they are missing a huge percentage of the population that could be shopping at their store."

Small companies today can't remain in the hiding when we talk about the ever-increasing number of consumers who vet brick-and-mortar businesses based on their online presence. Online presence not done well, or in some cases not done at all, could be keeping entrepreneurs from millions of customers – and rupees.

A website has functions which go beyond spreading awareness and making a sale. It allows businesses to distinguish themselves from their competitors, especially for customers who rely heavily on the internet to learn everything about a company. This makes a website one of the most critical business assets for sharing information, building credibility and standing out in crowded marketplaces.

To sum up, a website does these 3 things for your business effectively:

- Find Customers
- Build Credibility
- Gain Competitive advantage

- **Community Building**

What can't be measured can't be changed. It's a new norm that while creating a brand presence on social platforms, the top priority of any profile is to monitor and hack the growth of their follower base. Number tracking is key for any businesses to make sustainable progress. And with the help of these numbers creating a community around your brand is what will drive consumer loyalty. It's not only important to know who follows you, it is equally vital to strategically control who your brand follows back.

For local businesses community building is gaining importance as an essential tactic to execute. Pride is a vital parameter for showcasing how community takes interest and develops an integral approach to constructing your brand's identity. By following and engaging with local brands and native influencers, your brand establishes a presence both physically and mentally in the mind of the consumer. Do remember at all points audiences want to interact and build relationships with brands that are approachable and receptive to their feedback.

5 Benefits of Community Building

Continuous Improvement

Digital world has given customers a voice. Any new feature or product that a brand launches finds near-instant feedback via active online communities. This assists in shortening the cycle of innovation and helps companies make improvements very quickly, especially when it comes to digital products. Ultimately this elevates customer experience exponentially.

Measuring customer satisfaction

With an active online community, measuring customer satisfaction becomes much simpler.

By using online polls or qualitative surveys, brands can measure customer satisfaction levels. This applies not just to customer satisfaction of the product or service as a whole but could also apply to specific features or changes. Getting targeted customer satisfaction scores in real-time is possible with an engaged digital community.

Customer Retention

You can't be omnipresent. One has to get that straight. Having an active online community can help you solve that problem. Once you create a platform where people can learn from each other, are proactive, and help solve customer issues, you have figured out that problem solving tool which helps attract and retain new customers.

Airbnb is one of those start-ups that helps user's knowledge improve by learning from each other and enhancing their experience of the product.

Encourage Advocacy

Conventional methods of customer support have limited usage in today's ever evolving digital communities. Look beyond seeking to resolve customer issues. Engagement is the new buzz word which is buzzing and doing a lot for online communities. The biggest advantage is it allows brands to move towards customer advocacy. Customers' satisfaction and happiness are the focus of attention for brands while using online communities to their advantage. This changes brand perception to one that truly and deeply cares about its customers.

Jeff Bezos, CEO & Founder Amazon, famously said, "Your Brand is what people say about you when you are not in the room".

You will be surprised to know the same is measurable. True Fans, advocates, will either save your work or go ahead and share it and all of this can be measured on digital platforms. Capitalize on it!

Competition and need for Innovation

Small Businesses must serve a legitimate need in the community in order to survive and stand out from the rest. There is constant pressure to do better than their competitors. It's great for the marketplace and consumers when you have multiple small businesses all striving to be unique, innovative, and better. This increases the propensity of having more consumers warming up to local businesses.

How to build an effective community?

Start early, even if you are late its ok don't delay it even more, and have a long-term plan

Today community building starts as soon as the product or service is launched. Companies rely heavily on feedback and ways to improve the product as per consumer liking. This should be incorporated in your company's growth strategy at all points. At the same time, it's never too late to start building a community, even if you start with something as simple as a discussion forum. Of course, make sure you have a plan in place for how your community will change and grow with time.

Customer Reward Program

Many brands have forums where they enable their customers to send recipes that use their products. This encourages their customers to contribute creative content and other community members to benefit from this user-generated content. Many brands also recognize and reward customers for contributing content.

Offline efforts should go hand in hand with online communities

Offline efforts should be coupled with your online strategy. Activities like local meetups can really assist in cementing the efficacy of online communities. In today's online-first world, the right offline efforts can create a differentiator for a brand.

Digital communities, if and when utilized well, can really engage customers at a deep level and help transform the essence of the brand and its perception in the minds of users.

Having a thriving digital community and an effective offline strategy are not just desirable but are essential for businesses that want to get ahead in today's dynamic digital landscape.

#beenchanting

Strategize

YOU the Leader

CEOs, owners, founders are the brain of any company. They possess decision making powers which can shape the outcome of a company. But, how many of these leaders realize they are also being noticed, imitated, look up to by almost everyone in the company for inspiration. Not many of them are aware that it's much more than their brain that's been scanned. So, it's inevitable that the way leader walks, talks, dresses, communicates and does many other things is being observed with great intention. That makes it their responsibility to set an example for all those who aspire to be like them and the ones who draw inspiration from them. They are a brand, a much sort after one. And, like any other brand they need branding, constant and consistent. Brands don't become great because they happened, brands become great because that's what the intention behind it was, to make them great. Ground reality is that almost all the greats started the way you did. Greatness is not something that just happens; it's incredibly intentional.

(I) Personal Branding

A Brand has the power to attract, retain and multiply your business manifold. Isn't that what we want our company to do, show exponential growth. Often not taken seriously by small business owners, personal branding is like a superpower, if done well, it can not only save your world but can project you as a superhero to the rest of us. How seriously do we take brands? If today Bikaji launches a new variety of 'bhujia' and claims it to be the most tasteful in the market, most of us will not even question it and might as well commit to trying it. That's the power of a brand. Not only we perceive Bikaji to be good at making 'bhujia', but we also relate everything a good 'bhujia' has to offer with it. Bikaji is a manufacturing consultant for this mouthwatering product. That's the key. One has to not only become an expert in his/her domain, but one also has to highlight himself/herself as a consultant/expert in their field. As a result, people will start showing interest in whatever the 'Personal Brand' does in its domain, and the services will be looked at as something meaningful.

Personal Branding Kit

Website - Personal branding, unfortunately, is one aspect that most businesses tend to overlook. Most of our efforts are focused on ranking our company website higher on search engines, lead generation and conversion. All those things are, of course, essential to online success, but personal branding is just as important. If you want your audience to trust you, then you must learn the art of getting personal. Websites are available for as low as Rs 200, and platforms like google offer you free services which permit you to create a website with minimum effort. Capitalize on it before you fall behind in this race.

Facebook Page – Leverage FB's social media network and its incredible reach. It provides you validation in ways you can't possibly process. It helps you reach your target audience. We all know how difficult it is to reach out to audiences who are potential buyers for your product/service, an FB page can help you acquire these in the easiest way possible. Communication is another reason why FB page is so useful. It assists you in having effective communication with your potential customers/clients, again with relatable ease.

Blogs/Articles/Books – I will not focus on what monetary benefits these things can bring you, but just to highlight 1,00,000 copies of a book sold can bring you an income of 2 Crore approximately, given how you price it and how much you pay for the printing and advertising, and blah blah blah but that figure is a realistic one. Let's talk about other benefits like it projects you as a domain expert, it helps you garner a following, build a network, sell a product, express yourself and many more. Still thinking about the figure, then give it a shot.

"Leadership is about nurturing and enhancing." – Tom Peters, writer on business management practices.

(II) Networking

Network is net worth, not only an old adage but will remain true for as long as human interaction exists.

3 Types of networking for leaders

To be a successful leader, you need to build three different types of networks: Operational, Personal and Strategic:

1. Operational network

Your current work needs looking after. Your operational network involves people useful to you for fulfilling your current work tasks and responsibilities. These are the contacts you interact with on a daily basis for routine activities. Some managers and leaders do not reach beyond this network to become more successful leaders – keeping themselves trapped in technical and operational roles without achieving their full potential. It's a golden rule that networks and networking are crucial in both career and leadership transitions.

2. Personal network

There are many like-minded people outside your organization who need to be contacted to broaden your horizon beyond work. These can assist you in your personal growth and boost your advancement. You might know them through a mutual interest, but you can still leverage your acquaintance for business success. Always remember the world has to offer much more than can be seen and imagined. These contacts can provide important referrals, information, and, often, developmental support such as coaching and mentoring.

3. Strategic network

There are people who will be impressed by your actions and intentions and the great work you are doing. They would like to reach out to you and draw your attention to new business possibilities, new directions and new stakeholders necessary to achieve the critical objectives of your organization. According to Ibarra & Hunter, "The key to a good strategic network is leverage: the ability to marshal information, support, and resources from one sector of a network to achieve results in another."

Although active networking in all three areas is essential, the most important for a leader is strategic networking. Remember that it is part of a leader's job to network or build social capital as part of marshalling resources and achieving organizational goals.

"A robust leadership network helps provide access to people, information, and resources," says Curt Grayson, author of Leadership Networking: Connect, Collaborate, Create. "It goes beyond knowing or linking to lots of different people. It's about being able to use those connections wisely to solve problems and create opportunities."

(III) Celebrate

The world is one big celebration. Celebrating life is a sign of healthy living.

As leaders, it's easy and convenient to say to yourself, let's move forward and accomplish the next task, let's not allow anything to distract us. Especially when the wins are small in scale and impact, we often ignore those. The celebration honours the work and people who assisted you in accomplishing these tasks. It's an opportunity for you to show gratitude to the people who do it for you. Don't forget to celebrate, it's important.

By celebrating our success, we ensure the motivation levels increase, and we don't lose the drive that will carry us through to the next achievement. This is important at multiple levels; Individual, Organization as well as at community level. Take the time out to recognize the efforts that went into achieving that big success or even a modest win and do it authentically. Emphasize on what was accomplished, how it made a contribution, and why it's crucial.

Never forget to celebrate habits and qualities in addition to numbers. It's the culture of practices which will ensure the company continues to thrive in the right direction with the desired results.

5 Reasons you should celebrate success:

1. Develop a success mindset

Success breeds success. Success is a habit, and like all good habits, this too needs its fair share of looking after. Make sure you feed it enough mindfulness and consistency that it becomes your second nature.

2. Build your Confidence and Motivation

High performance teams are a function of confidence and motivation. A consistent dosage of these will set the cornerstones of how your teams perform in different situations. As a leader, you can't be omnipresent, and times when you can't contribute directly, you should make the most of your interactions to ensure your team feels motivated in the face of difficult situations.

3. Inspire People

The truth be told, inspiration is a leader's ornament. As a leader, you are a full-time inspirer. People are constantly feeding on your knowledge, energy, purpose, direction and things which you can't even fathom like your body language also counts. Remember, anyone can merely get the work done, the superstars, the leaders, however, do their work in a way that profoundly inspires others.

4. Happy Chemicals

There are four major chemicals in the brain that influence our happiness (DOSE):

Dopamine – Also known as chemical messenger and/or the Happiness drug. It generates a sense of satisfaction. Completing a task, striking tasks off your to do list, meeting a deadline gives one a rush of dopamine. It makes us feel good. Attaching a reward with tasks only further fuels the production of dopamine. A regular reward program for your employees can go a long way in ensuring enough chemical is produced for them to be excited to accomplish the work at hand daily.

Oxytocin - Assists us to be a social creature. It makes us empathize with others which helps us in creating close bonds. It gives us a warm feeling of being around someone you admire or like. Leaders busy enjoying their corner offices often miss out on inducing this feeling in their team members which can go a long way in ensuring the togetherness amongst employees.

Serotonin – Mood Regulator. 80 percent of serotonin exists in the gut and is governed by your state of hunger (yes, this is why you're hangry). It boosts your confidence and makes you feel great. It works both ways; give respect and a quality treatment to your team and receive the same in return. This helps maintain a balance of Serotonin which can boost the right amount of pride amongst the team members. This does lead to quality work and high performing teams.

Endorphins - When it comes to designing happiness, endorphins help you "power through." Endorphins allow one to push farther and harder even in the face of adversity. Some people love taking on challenging tasks which often leads to creation of superstars. When you spot a talent like this be rest assured to provide them enough endorphin as these individuals could well be tomorrows Leaders and Inspirers.

Use these chemicals to your benefit. Learn to boost them. Make time for exercise, laugh out loud, follow a hobby, make sure you are doing enough for these chemicals to work in your favor.

#beachemicalhacker

5 .Good News

A celebration isn't necessarily all about you. It allows others to join in with your celebration, be motivated and have a share in your success. A good point to remember is you have to recognize your success if you want others to do the same. How you do it is up to you – but do it and have some fun.

#perceptionbecomesreality

Strategize

Infinite Mindset

"Being the best is a loser strategy", no this is not the most controversial topic in the book, in fact it's an enlightening one. Simon Sinek, thinker, best-selling author and one of the most renowned modern gurus has an interesting take on Business strategies, and people love listening to him. If you haven't watched the video on golden circle, please do it asap, it's one of the best communication strategies you will ever discover.

Infinite Mindset, what is it? Simon says there are two types of games in business, finite and infinite. Finite has things figured out; players are known, their strategies, strengths, objectives and rules of the game all are pretty much figured out. On the other hand, infinite game has no boundaries or predictability; rules can change, players are in it to play on and on. It's driven by the spirit of innovation. The game of business by its very definition is an infinite game. The goal here is to keep getting better.

How to play this game?

1. Advance a bigger just cause – A Just Cause, put simply, is "a specific vision of a future state that does not yet exist; a future state so appealing that people are willing to make sacrifices in order to help advance towards that vision." The Just Cause

assists in creating an ecosystem that builds stronger support systems for entrepreneurs in their communities.

2. Foster Trusting Teams – It's important to promote values such as collaborative culture, shared vision, sustainable work in order to gain people's trust and confidence in building an organization which is strong, rooted and visionary.
3. Admire worthy rivals – It's important to study, applaud and acknowledge the work done by others in their field. Whether they are allies or rivals it doesn't matter, what matters is the intent and an opportunity to learn.
4. Practice existential flexibility – Steve Jobs once shared this thought with his team, "If you're not willing to blow up your own company, the market will do it for you." That popular advice led to Macintosh. You must have the capacity to make a profound strategic shift in order to advance your cause. The moment you discover something new that has the capacity to extend your cause you should be able to make the strategic shift to capitalize on it.
5. Courage to lead – Leadership is a way of life. It takes unbelievable courage to completely change the way we see the world. Goal is to look back at the end of our journey and feel the joy and pride of being part of something bigger than yourself. An example worth sharing is of BlockBuster (BB), movie rentals company in the US, which no longer exists. When Netflix was young and distributing subscriptions, BB CEO had asked his team to look into streaming services to which his team said 'No'

because 12% of BB's revenue use to come from late fee. Well, we know how that story turned out. BB is longer in the market and Netflix is ruling the roost.

#simonsayskeepgettingbetter

MBA

Marketing, Branding and Advertising

Marketing is the continuous efforts one makes towards building awareness for company's products and services. Every message about your company is part of your marketing. This includes all social media interactions, customer service, printed materials, websites, social media profile pages, and anything that contains your brand imagery.

Brand is the bundle of values and attributes that describe the unique value a company, product, or service delivers to customers, and the unique way of doing business that distinguishes its relationships with customers and other stakeholders. Brand is a perception of a company, product or service and just like a perception brand lives in the mind. This is intangible and that's what makes it powerful. Always remember Brand is not the company but a perception of it. Your company could be a small functioning entity but its image in people's mind is what differentiates it from the rest and can elevate it to the top. Mumbai's Dabba-Walas function like any other not so big company but the amount of respect they get for their work surpasses some of the biggest brands in India. Utilize it to your advantage.

Advertising is often considered as a subset of Marketing. Advertising is all about creating awareness and reaching new customers. Denise clarifies the difference between advertising and marketing this way: "Marketing is the big picture; advertising is a discrete effort."

Keep advertising and do so cleverly. Small businesses often don't have deep pockets to rub shoulders with bigger brands in the market but that doesn't mean they can't compete.

Consistency

I could not have signed off without this chapter. Probably the most known trait taught to us from childhood and many of us know how important it is, but do we know that if this is missing all that has been shared in this book stands on a weak footing. Doing a little everyday goes a long way in deciding how far you are from your intended target. Sachin Tendulkar and Brian Lara, probably two of the best batsmen and cricketers of the 1990s and 2000s era. One stands as probably the best cricketer to have played the game the other a fantastic batsman to have graced the game. Well, if you go by stats there is little to choose between the two. In fact, at one point in their career they were considered equal. Although many bowlers have gone on record to say Lara was a bigger threat, that says a lot about Lara's aura. To be honest, even I believe Lara was more fun to watch over Tendulkar, and probably better. But, the history, suggests otherwise. What made Sachin leave Brian far behind when the difference between the two was nominal? Consistency! Sachin's consistency on and off the field, staying grounded and giving his best inspite of all the distractions, was so remarkable that he lasted for a tenure longer and more fruitful than Brian. The record speaks for itself.

No matter what the challenges are do ensure you keep ticking towards your target; how far it may seem, how difficult it may look, at the end of the day it's your consistency that will get you over the line.

Acknowledgement

The world becomes better with sharing and caring. I want to thank all the people who have had a positive impact on my life. My parents, my gurus, my idols and ever so competitive business world for teaching me lessons constantly. The growing will to contribute towards the knowledge and growth of others has been a big reason for writing this book. I wish to continue on the path of growth and would like to request all the readers of this book to spread joy and knowledge, and do not forget to write back to me about the book. Your feedback will help me evolve. Thanks.

About the Author

Ashwini Walia is a Business Coach and Mentor; he has been assisting and transforming SMEs for over 10 years now. He has worked in industries such as Manufacturing, Education, F&B and Fashion, and helped companies attain exponential progression in less than 12 months. He works on the principle of Automating sales and marketing for sustainable results. He holds degrees in Engineering and Business Management from premier institutes in India and aboard. Ashwini is on a mission to educate and facilitate small and medium businesses in India with a contemporary approach towards business. He has made sales and marketing very easy and efficient for small businesses which can further assist businesses in scaling with less expenditure and more sustainable results.

A note from the Author

As I am writing this book, we are in the midst of a horror named Covid – 19 which has already taken thousands of lives world over. Countless businesses have been shut, countless jobs have been lost, and the future once again is very uncertain. It's daring to think positive in these testing times. So, what's the plan of action? Sit back and wait for the time to pass. Well, a lot of leaders are suggesting the same. Not a bad choice but I firmly believe there is a lot we can do and achieve even when the chips are down. I have wanted to write this book for years, and finally, here I am finishing the thing which has been pending for a while now. I am quite certain we all have such passions lying somewhere in the closet which can come out and take shape for good. After all, every disaster is an opportunity to do something revolutionary. I urge one and all to gather the courage and the will to fight these difficult times with the vigour only humans are known for. There resides a champion in each one of us; lets encourage it to come out and make a difference.

#neverletadisastergotowaste